1

The

Language of
Fungi & Flowers

(A collection of poems)

Flor Ana

Kate,
thank you
for your support♡
may these
poems
inspire
you

Published 2021

1st edition / 01

ISBN: 9798733509716

Independently published

Cover art by Flor Ana

www.littleearthflower.com

Table of Contents

II. of Flowers… 65

dedicated to the

dreamers

who look at nature

in awe of its beauty,

dream of flower fields,

wish upon stars

and appreciate all that

mother earth

has to offer

Reader, you hold here a piece of my heart and all of my wild love for nature. May it encourage you to step outside and see all the beauty this planet has to offer. There's absolutely nothing like it and I'm grateful for it all.

Of Fungi

Nature alone is antique, and the oldest art a mushroom.

Thomas Carlyle

If you've ever stumbled upon a mushroom

If you've ever stumbled upon a mushroom
in the forest,
in the garden,
in your backyard,
did you fall down the rabbit hole
alongside Alice
and the wonders of Wonderland?
Were you intrigued by their shape
or their magical powers?
Perhaps, what most intrigued you was
their intelligence,
their ability to rule the ground
without humans ever knowing a single thing
about their reign,
the way they send messages to the trees
millions of spores, millions of seeds
of knowledge
to everything in their vicinity,
some deadly,
some beautiful,
some kaleidoscopic.

If you ever stumble upon a mushroom

in the forest,

in the garden,

in your backyard,

be like Alice,

falling down the rabbit hole,

discovering Wonderland.

Both growing — expanding the mind

and shrinking — diminishing the doubts.

Do not consume all you see,

do not forget the deadly,

but simply

be

in awe.

Alaskan Gold

Phaeolepiota aurea

you're stained gold

as if all you've seen

are sunsets

sewn

by the sun

in the mountains

abundant in Alaska

I've yet to meet you

in real life

but I know a man

who ventured the Alaskan

wilderness

and like your name

that man is

Alaskan Gold

skin stained golden

by the sunset scenes

in the mountains

Angel Wings

Pleurocybella porrigens

among dead conifers[1], i see angel wings emerging,
leading the trees to a new life
through a staircase of white
a new beginning

flesh thin and fragile
innocent and celestial,
souls led through the universe to a new home
even in death, the trees know they are loved

Bear's Head

Hericium abietis

have you ever seen
the leaves
of a willow tree,
swaying in the wind
tall and green in the spring?

now, picture one dressed in white,
smaller,
clusters of spines
hanging like icicles
from branches' tips

no longer are you picturing
a willow,
but a
Bear's Head mushroom
instead

still one with nature,
connected to the universe,
to the trees themselves,
to us

mushrooms and trees

are bridges between

when looking

with brand new eyes

Bleeding Hydnellum

Hydnellum peckii

strawberries and cream
summer berry pudding
cherries black and red
donut jelly filling

you remind me of childhood summers
bruises and mosquito bites
blood oozing from innocent cuts
strawberry milk filled nights

forbidden fruit you bleed
red droplets when your fresh
like what lies beneath our skin
red worlds under our flesh

Blewit

Clitocybe nuda

lilac-tinged, pale and purple fuzz
i found you
in debrised woods

i'm sorry for picking you
planting chaos in your world
i know, i blew it

but i was intrigued
by your majestic purple complexion
enticing and of fairy tales

you forgave me
yet when i saw you again
i left you still

admired you with just my eyes
enjoying the moment we shared
that i still have memorized

Blue-green Anise Mushroom

Clitocybe odora

i've never had a mushroom cookie
not one shaped like a mushroom
or one made with a mushroom
but when i do for the first time
i will use *blue-green anise*
and eat it with my tea
in a field of wildflowers
on a sunny, breezy day
that makes the flowers sway
and i won't know if the sweet smell
is coming from the flora or the fungi
but what i do know is that i
will be at peace
in my own version of wonderland
with pen and paper in hand
trying my best to describe it all

Chanterelle

Cantharellus cibarius

charming chanterelle

white

yellow foot

scaly

and blue

it's nice to finally meet you

nature's finest

your apricot aroma

peppered and lightly fruited taste

makes mouths water as you melt onto the tongue

each spoonful a creamy delicacy

you truly are a food of the gods

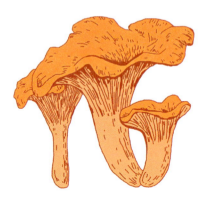

Cloudy Clitocybe

Clitocybe nebularis

they call you skunk for your obnoxious odor yet

your name reminds me of the daylight sky

clouds

cumulus and cumulonimbus

altostratus and altocumulus

white on sunny days

gray when the rains

come

cotton on the ground

your steps make no sound

but I appreciate your smell of rain from miles away

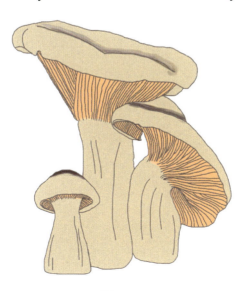

Death Cap

Amanita phalloides

Decomposition

that's what's to come
when I think and see
you, *death cap*

I accept death
when it's to come
in all its pale green, greenish-yellow glory

like your veil, *death cap*
one day, a veil will cover my eyes
and it'll be some time

before I am born again

Deer Mushroom

Pluteus cervinus

Oh deer,
how I wish you were here.
That day when I found you upon this magical sphere,
I didn't touch you, but not out of fear.

I found you while wandering, emerging from the ground
and when I saw you, the world made no sound.
Your cap stood before me like a domed crown
and I was amazed, in awe and spellbound.

I took your picture, posted it in black and white.
The original photograph now lost to the light
and when I posted of you, it was about the fight
for legalization of your species' psychedelic might.

Oh deer,
how I hold you and yours so dear,
wishing to find you whenever you're near
because when I do, I see the world so clear
and you erase the veils that instill us with fear.

Destroying Angel

Amanita ocreata

it's time for the veil to be lifted
it's time for the world to be shifted

but please don't ingest the destroying angel
for it's properties are not evangel

let us use its symbolic pure white color
to lift the world's veil
if we use our light for good,
the world *can* be good, without fail

let this lethal species be just a representation
for a world beautiful beyond imagination

if it was meant to be eaten, why would it be destroying angels?
if we were meant to live like this, why would we be so unhappy?

Earthstar

Astraeus hygrometricus

a constellation of earthstars fill the ground
looking like little humans with domed hats
or decayed sunflowers or starfish
or some other undiscovered creature

i'm reminded of childhood
collecting pokemon cards
simply for aesthetics
wanting the coolest of the bunch

a constellation of earthstars
cover the ground
and i picture little mushroom people
at work
out for lunch
having tea
gardening
living their lives underground
through a network of mycelium[2]

how little do most earthborn know about the earthstars

Fairy Ring Mushroom

Marasmius oreades

pretty little mushroom ladies
wear their bonnets and dance
in a circle in the grass
and we call it a fairy ring

portal to a different world, they say
don't step inside the fairy ring

but i don't want to step inside
i want to dance among
the magical women in white
ruffled, layered dresses
barefoot
feeling the grass
beneath their feet
dancing to a song
its rhythm so sweet

pretty little mushroom ladies
wear their bonnets and dresses
twirling in the grass
and i want to join in on the fairy ring dance

Fly Amanita

Amanita muscaria

ah yes, the magic mushroom
the shaman's choice
the inspiration for countless trips
and the story of santa claus and his flying reindeer

your mystical mythology
is almost as intoxicating as your properties
and i know once someone stumbles upon you
there's no going back to the reality of before

you're the forbidden fruit
off the tree of knowledge
and to consume you would
change everything

in fact, it was through you
our ape-like ancestors
discovered their fingers,
unlocking the potential
for all we are today

Hawk Wing

Sarcodon imbricatum

scales of sacred geometry
are tattooed
onto your flesh

you're nature's perfect example
of imperfect perfection in patterns

your flesh is brittle
and you can vary in color
like your sisters
and brothers

to stare at you
is to stare into the face
of a mesmerizing
mind-altering trip
only understood by those
in awe of your beauty

Hideous Gomphidius

Gomphidius glutinosus

you're owed an apology

for whoever named you

hideous

when truly

you are

beautiful

your bright yellow stalk

is like the sun

warm and vibrant

and your

rosy pink complexion

is my favorite

because i see your

blush

at the thought of

being beloved

Honey Mushroom

Armillaria mellea

honey honey

mushroom sweet

your golden tones paint

sunsets for me

clusters painted

upon a tree

the perfect pairing

to my cup of tea

honey honey

kiss me sweet

i look for you

beneath my feet

in my glass of

whiskey neat

finding you on hikes

is the most rewarding treat

Indigo Milk Cap

Lactarius indigo

have you ever stopped to think

about how unnatural the color blue is.

rare in nature, yet we see it all around:

blue morpho butterflies, blue jays and even ladybugs

we can find blue among mushrooms too.

isolated indigo, i know i love you so.

bluish features and bright blue juice.

virtually unmistakeable and easy to choose.

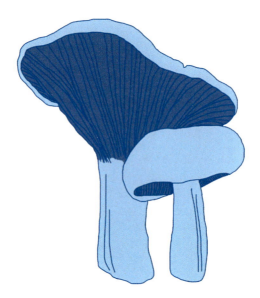

Liberty Cap

Psilocybe semilanceata

Hallucinogenic

, you are

So, I decided

to make

this poem

hallucinate

too

Hundreds of fractals

*(in brown, dark gray, purple-brown,
whitish, bluish, olive)*

Clusters of words

All

alluding

to you.

Meadow Mushroom

Agaricus campestris

meadow mushrooms
gills blush-pink and chocolate-brown
cover the grassy alpine ground

flesh unstained when rubbed or cut
a mushroom rendition of a hazelnut

they dance in groups and rings in grazed pastures
sometimes showing off their pink bottoms,
but for no masters

their taste is a popular favorite,
especially among the English
but sometimes their appearance
may be hard to distinguish

while meadow mushrooms provide a tasty treat
misidentification may cause you to miss a beat

Morel

Morchella esculenta

While walking the river valley,

I stumbled upon a honey-combed morel in the sandy soil.

Backdrop of dead leaves camouflaging her,

I would have missed her if not for her pits and ridges,

standing out like the strangest spring flower I'd ever seen.

Upon finding her,

my lucky four-leafed clover,

I realized she was everywhere.

Dozens of morels hidden amongst the woods,

scattered in all directions,

awaiting those willing to truly open their eyes

and see them

It made me think.

This brain-like fungi would not have appeared

before my eyes

had *my* brain decided to filter her out.

Experience may just be determined

by what we can perceive,

and oh, how I wish to see it all.

That way, next time I'm walking the river valley,
amongst the woods,
I'll find the morel of the story more quickly.
If not, I'll just continue
walking a forest of morels without ever seeing them,
and that, that would truly be a shame.

Northern Red-dye

Dermocybe sanguinea

Among the tall blades of grass
in a forest of nature's finest flowers and fungi
lives a garden fairy

She awakens before dawn,
dew drops soaking her bare feet
as she sets out in search of spruce trees

Once the trees tower over her,
she begins searching the ground
for red mushrooms just a little larger than she is

Finally, she sees four red-orange stalks
and knows she's found what she's looking for

Her face brightens, a smile emerges
almost as wide and beautiful as her wings
and she pulls with all her might to unroot
the northern red-dye

Hands the color of blood, she exhales triumphantly

dragging a single mushroom
back to her home

She begins to chop away at her finding,
painting a canvas with her fingers,
the whole thing looking like a crime scene

Yet, on closer inspection,
what you find is a fairy
painting a rose with her own bare hands
from the paint of a mushroom

the most natural way to make art

Orange Peel Fungus

Aleuria aurantia

Golden Fairy Cup[3],

I wonder how many times

people passed you by

on their spring and summer hikes

in the mountainous woods

thinking you were just a simple

discarded orange peel

instead of a complex orange entity.

Parrot Mushroom

Hygrocybe psittacina

Among the moss
in woods and bogs,
you'll find a me
saying pretty on repeat
~ like a parrot ~

Even though I am shy,
perhaps this is why
my pine green colors
attract many lovers
~ I know I am pretty ~

And I know if you
just did the same too
and believed in your beauty,
achieved your self-loving duty
~ you'd believe in yourself and know your worth,
seeing you're of the most beautiful things on this earth ~

Violet Cort

Cortinarius violaceus

It's not often in nature

you see something deep purple.

Blue itself is a rarity,

but deep purple

is a memorable find.

One that transports you

to a world of witches and magic and all in between

or perhaps it's already here

but goes unseen.

There are many other purple species of

Cortinarius,

but none are like the

Violet Cort,

the one that distorts

your reality and makes you believe

in the things unknown, unseen

in a world of wonders

where it's possible to communicate with thunder.

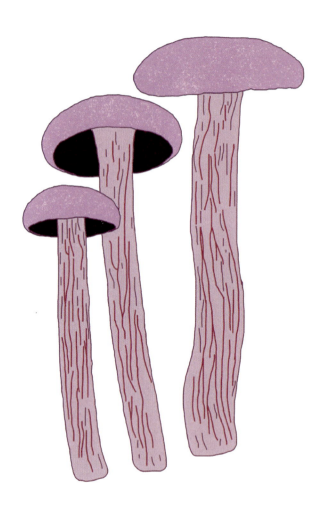

Western Amethyst Laccaria

Laccaria amethysteo-occidentalis

amethyst mushroom or amethyst crystal
the higher vibrations of both beneficial
helping release all that is superficial
enhancing a connection that is spiritual

purple, protective, and purifying
its properties will make you feel like your flying
how these cosmic creations came to be is mystifying
but knowing they're here is so gratifying

one you can eat and one you can wear
both bring a calmness to the light air
with the power to transport you elsewhere
my love for amethysts i want to declare

Witch's Hat

Hygrocybe conica

witches of the ground
roam mossy woods
in their pointed
bright yellow, orange or red caps

they blacken with age,
but they use their spores to
transfer their magic
their knowledge
their energy
through a network of
mycelium and air
ready to once more
begin nature's cycle

Woodland Agaricus

Agaricus silvicola

odor of crushed flesh

sweet

like almond extract or anise

fill the air

as the creatures of the forest

have a tea party for an unbirthday

woodland agaricus cake

baked to perfection

drizzled in chocolate maple

topped with yellow spots and flowers

the hares and bears

and mice with their wears

all celebrate their existence

living another day

under the natural

forest canopy

Mycophile

Mycophile:
A devotee
of mushrooms

I never thought I'd be here
Yet here I am
Guidebook in hand
In search of one of nature's
Most unique and intelligent creations

So like humans and so not
Growing from the places of rot
Making life out of death
And bring death with one breath
The peculiarities are spectacular

From false claims of allergies
To searching for you
On every tree, blade of grass or soil-rich dirt
I am proud to say I devote myself to being happy
And I enjoy finding mushrooms
And learning about their ways

Because if an organism can communicate

In silence

Underground

And affect so much life

In both chaos and order

How can we *not* be intrigued?

How can we *not* be in awe?

Of Flowers

She wore flowers in her hair
and carried magic secrets in her eyes.

Arundhati Roy

For those who stop and look at flowers

for those who stop and look at flowers
curious of the creatures
that lay their
many legs and wings
on their soft petals

for those who stop and look at flowers
breathing in their sweet aroma
or perhaps taking photographs
trying to find their unique names
how they exist in such a peculiar world

for those who stop and look at flowers
grateful for their existence
and remember that they too
are flowers
beautiful and intricate and full of wonder

Arnica

Arnica montana

you warm my skies.
your yellow petals
are like a kiss from the sun,
speaking stories of the wise.

your leaves, soft and hairy,
calming the pain,
remind me of your cousin, sunflower,
another perennial[4] for the sun to marry.

poisonous you are,
but in small diluted doses,
you're angelic, like the mountains you come from,
in the distance, looking like night stars.

Aster

Symphyotrichum

Attention,

Stars and planets of the cosmos,

There's a bright rayed amethyst flower on

Earth, cultivating love and wisdom,

Ready to return to the altars of the gods

Bellflower

Campanula

With gratitude,
I ring the bells of joy
for the blessings in my life.

I gift the universe
bellflowers, partly purple,
their bells ringing throughout the cosmos.

Calla Lily

Zantedeschia aethiopica

Charming and beautiful,

As other flowers are in the garden

Lovely is your name, the

Language of feminine beauty

Alas, no perennial is like you

Listening to your bells,

I know you are extraordinary

Living in the universe in an array of colors:

Yellow, orange, pink, rose, lavender and dark maroon

(and my favorite: white with yellow spadix[5])

Calendula

Calendula officinalis

my marigold mother
your bright orange petals
fill my days
with wondrous warmth,
all-encompassing

self-willed sunshine, fearless fire
your essence is enchanting,
encouraging us to
communicate clearly,
unafraid to speak our thoughts

Carnation

Dianthus caryophyllus

it's time for the coronation
vases filled with colorful carnations
the crowning will soon commence

it's time for new beginnings
the buried beauty and its winnings
basking in good sense

it's the taste of triumphant traditions
as musicians tickle the tempo with new transitions
hoping the tetrarch will give them more than cents

it's the longing for love and life
lasting longer than loosestrife[6]

Chicory

Cichorium intybus

common chicory
bee and bubble
alas, allow me
to pay my praise

nonnative innocence
sweet species
of bright blue
you brighten all of my days

perseverant and protecting,
you are the flower of fairytales
woody, perennial herbaceous plant
you are a member of the dandelion family

grounded into coffee
brewed and enjoyed 'au lait'
lacking the caffeine that makes me jitter
a blessed delivery of alchemy

cichorium intybus
perhaps otherworldly

your uses vary

like the colors of your petals

yet you can grow

along roadsides

wild and naturalized

deserving sapphire medals

Chrysanthemum

Chrysanthemum morifolium

I remember reading

the story of *Chrysanthemum*,

how the little mouse

learned to love her mellow-flower name.

It wasn't until now

that I realized

she and I were, in ways,

one and the same.

Growing up,

I too questioned my own name.

Beautiful in my mother tongue,

yet distastefully said by nonnatives.

Chrysanthemum, Chrysanthemum:

"Happiness, Love,

Longevity and Joy."

That is me, too,

and yet, I am coy.

I am in

every flower.

Just like

every flower

is in me,
united together
for all eternity.

Blessed with beautiful names
we all are,
decided long ago
when we were still
the dust of stars;
like *Chrysanthemum*,
I too
love my name
and that is something
no one can ever
take or change.

Cosmos

Cosmos bipinnatus

imagine

a cosmo floating in the cosmos

maybe

not just one

but dozens

of cosmos in our cosmos

like stardust

each a different color

each a different shade

blossoming infinitely

only adding beauty

to an already

beautiful

universe

Daffodil

Narcissus

the universe

has given us

daffodils

white with yellow and peach corona[7]

a sign

of new beginnings

spring

shown in its six trumpet-shaped petals

a rebirth

is coming soon

guided

by the blooming amaryllis[8] awaiting cultivation

Daisy

Bellis perennis

Darling daisy,

my April flower,

every time I stumble upon

your white petals

in fields of green

between the cracks of sidewalks

tangled in the blades

I can't help but feel grateful

something about your light calls to me

and reminds me of the feeling of being free

Elderflower

Sambucus

in times of sickness
you brought me health

through sniffles and sore throats
the berries of your flowers
sweet and tart
nursed me

your petals white as snow
your fruit purple as darkness
medicine of mother earth
a friend to those in need
when something foreign enters their bodies

how I ate
of your elder wisdom
in gelatinous form
every day
in sickness and in health

Evening Primrose

Oenothera

good evening primrose

nice to see you here in

the midnight garden

your open yellow petals like

miniature moons

amongst your leaves

or perhaps you are like

the stars

shining in the night sky

illuminating the way

for the nocturnal creatures

that wish to see your beauty

while they go about their routines

basking in the twilight sounds

that put us humans to peaceful sleep

Forget Me Not
Myosotis

a testament
to our love
written in the cosmos
displayed on earth
through mouse-eared flowers
in clear and charming sky-blue with yellow throats

a symbol
of true love
never to be forgotten
everlasting in the universe
like the stars in the night sky
expanding for miles and miles without end

forget me not, true love

Hawthorn
Crataegus

hawthorn, quickthorn, thornapple, may-tree
thank you for bringing my grandmother to me
on a may day she was born long ago
living a life i can't get to know

your white petals, peppered in pink and black
represent love and protection — things i don't lack
for my grandmother has blessed me with her love
as pure as your white petals that hang from above

you're a tree of enchantment, bursting with magic
looking like snow — a beautiful fabric
thank you for who you birthed in a 1940 may
a grandmother's love is more than words can say

Hollyhocks
Alcea

Tower of flowers
You stand
Tall
Like this poem
Reaching up
Into the sky
Wanting to
Be kissed by the sun

Your midsummer bloom
Comes in
A variety of colors
Maroons and peaches
Attracting
Butterflies and bees
You're fruitful

Your roots
Sink
Into the ground
Your petals
Reach
Into the heavens

When I
Grow up
I want
To be
Like you

Honeysuckle
Lonicera

I see you there
between the twining vines
looking like fairies
resting on the leaves
inviting others in
with your sweet smell of honey

Lavender
Lavandula

Lavender,
I drew you first

because enough poems
have been written about
your mildly sweet floral scent
herbal and balsamic undertones
that with each inhalation relaxes

Lavender,
I drew you first

because your soft pastel purples
and growing green stems
were too beautiful not to envision
on a piece of paper or computer screen
almost aromatic to your admirers

Lavender,
I drew you first

because I didn't know
what words would be enough
to say the way what you've made me feel
the casual companion you've been
in oils, in my tea or on my chapped lips

what I would do to lay with you in the fields
and bask in the sun's rays

Lily
Lilium

Born of breast milk
You were the dedicated flower
But who would've known
That love wouldn't last the hour

Zeus was a god, but he was no saint
Yet your white petals are meant
To symbolize stainlessness; purity
But when Venus came and went

Jealousy lingered
In her heart
And with a pistol at your center
Your freshness fell apart

Hera, your creator
Meant for you to be of aid
In Hercules' immortality
His fate and free will weighed

And from your milk
The Milky Way was created
Splashed across the heavens
An event that now seems fated

And from those drops
Somehow you came
To fall upon the earth
Lily became your name

And now, here,
We know you as you are
A white delicate flower
That came from the stars

Morning Glory
Ipomoea

morning glory
you september sapphire flower
mary oliver wrote about you
laid with you in the fields
as you held your head high
in the cornstalks
and you talked with her of
the reaper's story
and you shared with her
the truth of his life
of his endless work
of how connected it is
and while she wrote about you
somber
a little unreliable in your
almost-human-like sway
i see you and think
morning glory
you september sapphire flower of mortality
blooming and dying every day
renewal is your name
rising
in blue and dark-blue
beautiful and bright
inspiring
born again
every day

Orchid
Orchidaceae

the favorite
of the women
in my family
grandmother, mother, and sister

you are
divinely woman
living in an array of colors

white, elegant and innocent
pink, pure feminine

yellow like my mother's golden hair in the sun
and red like the bold blood that runs down our legs

purple, royal and admirable
orange, full of charisma and enthusiasm

exotic
like the women
unknown and bloodlined
that roam this earth

mystifying
with our fertility, virility, and femininity

Petunia
Petunia × *atkinsiana*

petunia
my *Brave Petunia*
like Irian
i receive you as my name
unexpectedly

but unlike *Dragonfly*
this name did not come from a Rose
but rather a piece of technology
somehow still as magical

i had not considered myself brave
but here we are
two sides of the same coin

i am serenity
you are anger
and yet we both are
mysterious
whimsical
an enigma in and of itself

you come to me in
purples and pinks
fuschias and fiery reds
yet it is yellow
i feel closest to
yellow like the sun
warmed by the sun

as i try to warm those around me, those i love

Poppy
Papaver

how i'm glad
to have
met you
August flower

you've forever
changed
my life
and for the better

thank you
for the man
you birthed
in late summer

a soulmate
a friend
a partner
a lover

you're red
like the love
that courses
our veins

giving us
a high
spiritual love
that remains

everlasting
beyond life
and death
evermore

Rose
Rosa

a rose for a rose — and everyone is a rose
so roses fill the garden
reds, whites, yellows, pinks
all scattered around the world — all pardoned
each with their own thorns and stories
petals bruised, withering and blossoming
each and every one beautiful in their own way
with lives that are all so promising

Sunflower
Helianthus

sunflower
to me
you are
love's incarnate
warming the heart
and brightening the days

Tulip
Tulipa

i know spring is here
when your aroma
fills the air
and i can't escape the sight
of your vibrant colors
never could you have too many tulips

you're the symbol of perfection
deep love and admiration
and how i wish to one day roam your fields
in a summer dress and brimmed hat
barefoot as i feel the damp soil
between my toes
and we both look up at the sun
in awe of life and mother earth and the fact
that we can both be here
experiencing it all together

Wallflower
Erysimum

I look in the mirror and see,
looking at me, a wallflower
pink and purple and orange beauty
small, but bursting with power

some may call me introverted,
but I reckon I'm a daydreamer
the universe, with me, has flirted
enlightening me with conscious fever

bright as the orange petals
that grow from the stems
choosing to never settle,
a new journey begins

Anthophile

Anthophile:
an organism
who visits flowers
or
a person
who loves flowers

kind of the same,
don't you think?

all admirers
of the blossoming petals
alive in an array
of colors, shapes and sizes

kind of like us,
don't you think?

living
our lives through our eyes
withering and blossoming
dying and being reborn
with each rotation
of the sun
which keeps us
here
alive

we may be more like flowers
than we think

Language used in Of Fungi and Of Flowers

Conifers [1]***:*** *Trees bearing cones and needle-like leaves that are typically evergreen.*

Mycelium [2]***:*** *The vegetative part of fungi that consists of a network of fine white filaments and helps absorb nutrients from the environment.*

Golden Fairy Cup [3]***:*** *Another name for the Orange Peel Fungus.*

Perennial [4]***:*** *A type of flowering plant that grows in multiple seasons.*

Spadix [5]***:*** *The spike of tiny flowers closely arranged around a fleshy axis, typically located at the center.*

Loosestrife [6]***:*** *Tall plants that bear upright spikes of flowers that can typically sustain themselves for over 20 years as a monoculture.*

Corona [7]***:*** *A crown-shaped appendage of certain flowers, such as daffodils.*

Amaryllis [8]***:*** *The family of flowers from which daffodils come from.*

Floral symbolism described in Of Flowers

Arnica: Aligns with the sun and the element of fire.

Aster: Named after the Greek word for "star" because of its resemblance.

Bellflower: Gratitude; often given as a thank you.

Calla Lily: Broadly symbolizes purity and holiness.

Calendula: A symbol of sunshine and fire.

Carnation: A symbol of luck and admiration.

Chicory: Perseverance.

Chrysanthemum: Love, happiness, longevity and joy.

Cosmos: Peace.

Daffodil: Rebirth and new beginnings.

Daisy: A symbol of innocence; the April flower.

Elderflower: Good health and prosperity; protection from harm.

Evening Primrose: Sweet memories.

Forget Me Not: True love; fidelity.

Hawthorn: Tree of enchantment; the May flower.

Hollyhocks: Ambition and protection.

Honeysuckle: A symbol of happiness and affection.

Lavender: Serenity and grace.

Lily: Devotion and purity.

Morning Glory: The mortality of life.

Orchid: Fertility, virility and sexuality.

Petunia: Anger; the September flower.

Poppy: August flower.

Rose: All roses symbolize God's love in the world at work. Different colored roses symbolize different things.

Sunflower: Adoration, loyalty and longevity.

Tulip: Deep love and clarity.

Wallflower: Faithfulness in adversity.

Acknowledgments

I do not encourage the consumption of any mushrooms discussed in this poetry collection. Please do your own research on the edibility of each individual consumable mushroom.

"Northern Red-dye" was inspired by a daydream.

The poem "Chrysanthemum" was inspired by Kevin Henkes' children's book *Chrysanthemum*, which I loved as a child.

I'd like to dedicate the poem "Daisy" to my father who is my April flower.

I'd like to dedicate "Hawthorn" to my grandmother who has always been my rock.

The poem "Lily" was inspired by Greek mythology and the story of Hera and Zeus.

"Morning Glory" was inspired by and responds to Mary Oliver's poem titled "Morning Glories."

I'd like to dedicate "Orchid" to the women in my family and in my heart. Primarily, I'd like to dedicate it to my sister, who adores orchids and introduced them to our family many moons ago, and my mother, who nurtures them whenever we have them in the house.

The poem "Petunia" was inspired by Ursula K. Le Guin's short story *Dragonfly*, which discusses the importance of names. "Brave Petunia" was my given name in the PictureThis app for distinguishing flowers.

I want to mention David Arora's book *All That The Rain Promises and More...* Thank you for being the ultimate pocket guide to western mushrooms and helping me find the inspiration to not only illustrate the mushrooms in this book, but also learn about all the different species.

I want to thank my loved ones who have continued to support me on my journey of being a writer and author. You all fill my life with love and joy and I am eternally grateful for the support and love I receive.
I want to thank my laptop for not giving up on me while illustrating countless flowers and mushrooms and overheating most of the way through it.

Reader, I also deeply want to thank you for reading my words. May they inspire you and help you in any way possible. May they awaken in you a love for nature that runs deep and remind you of the beauty that it is to be alive.

Flor Ana Mireles is an artist, writer, editor, poet and singer, born in Cuba and raised in Miami, FL. She debuted as an indie author with her self-published poetry collection *Perspective (and other poems)* and continues to inspire others through her work.

She continues to create art and wants others to know that they have the power to achieve their wildest dreams. They just need to put in the work.

You can find her at @littleearthflower on Instagram.

For other works and projects by Flor, go to www.littleearthflower.com

Made in the USA
Monee, IL
24 June 2021